Coloring Pages For Kids Deep Sea Creatures Coloring Book

Coloring Books for Kids

By Gala Publication

Published by:

Gala Publication

ISBN-13: 978- 1508659464
ISBN-10: 150865946X

©Copyright 2015 – Gala Publication

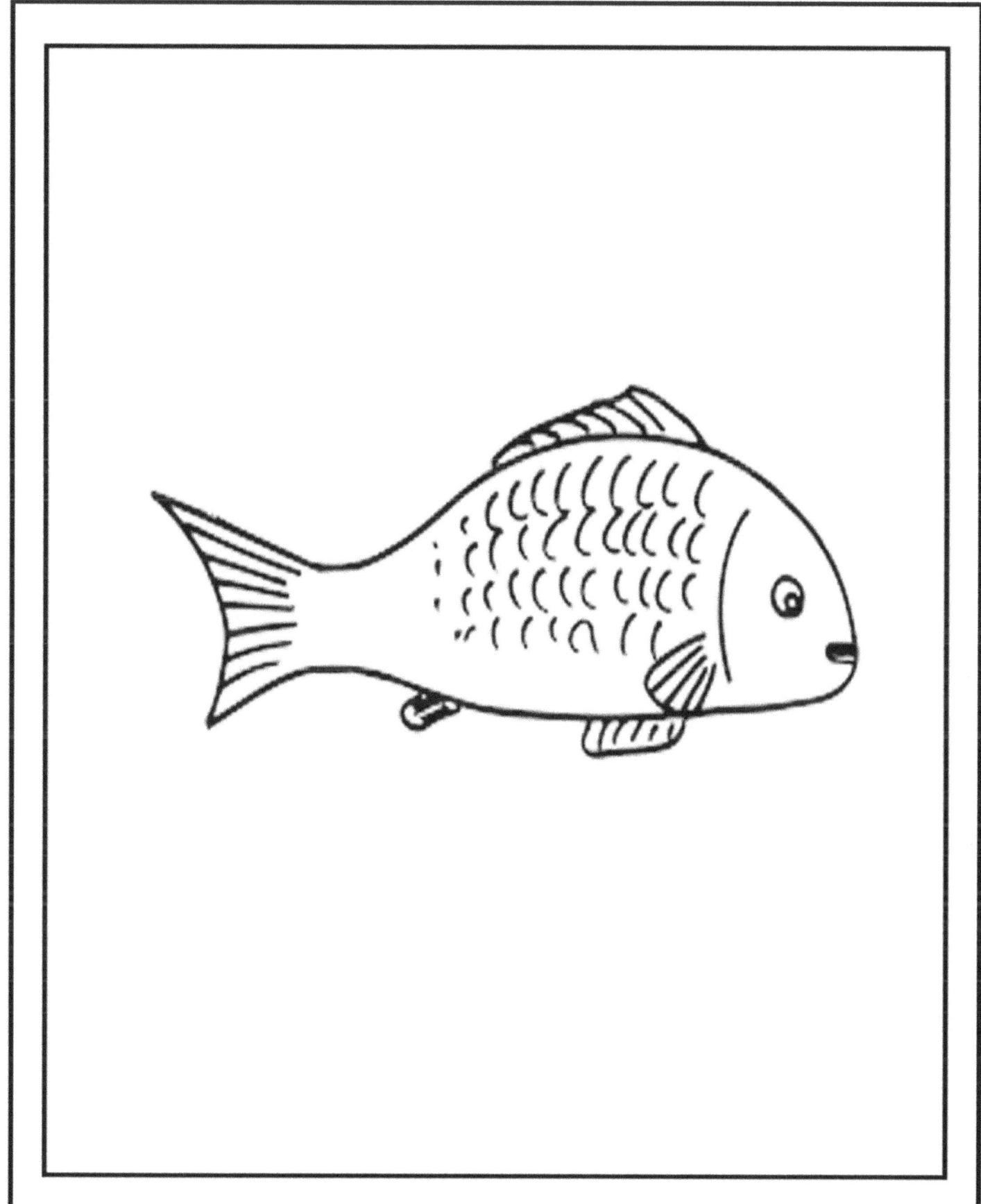

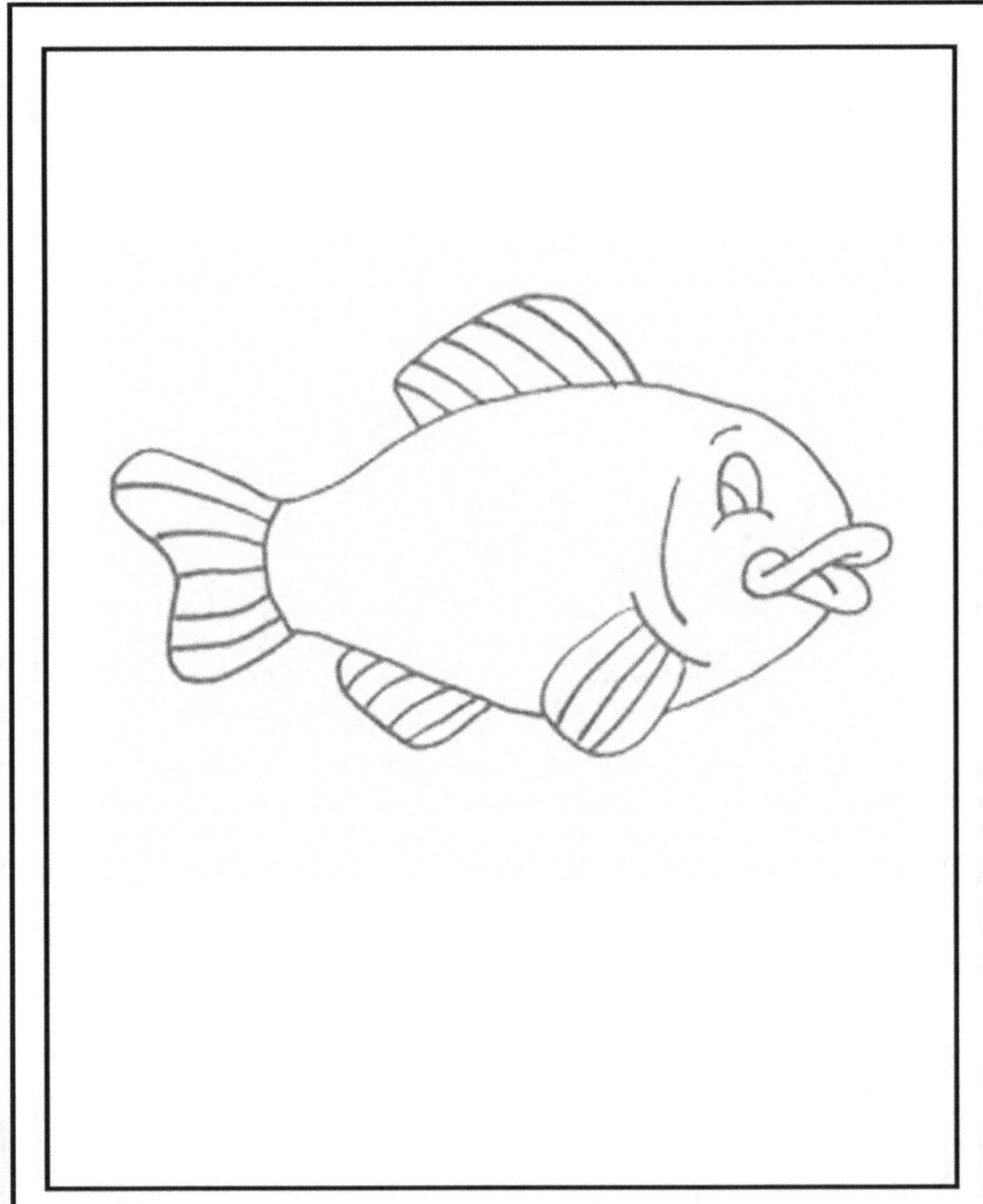

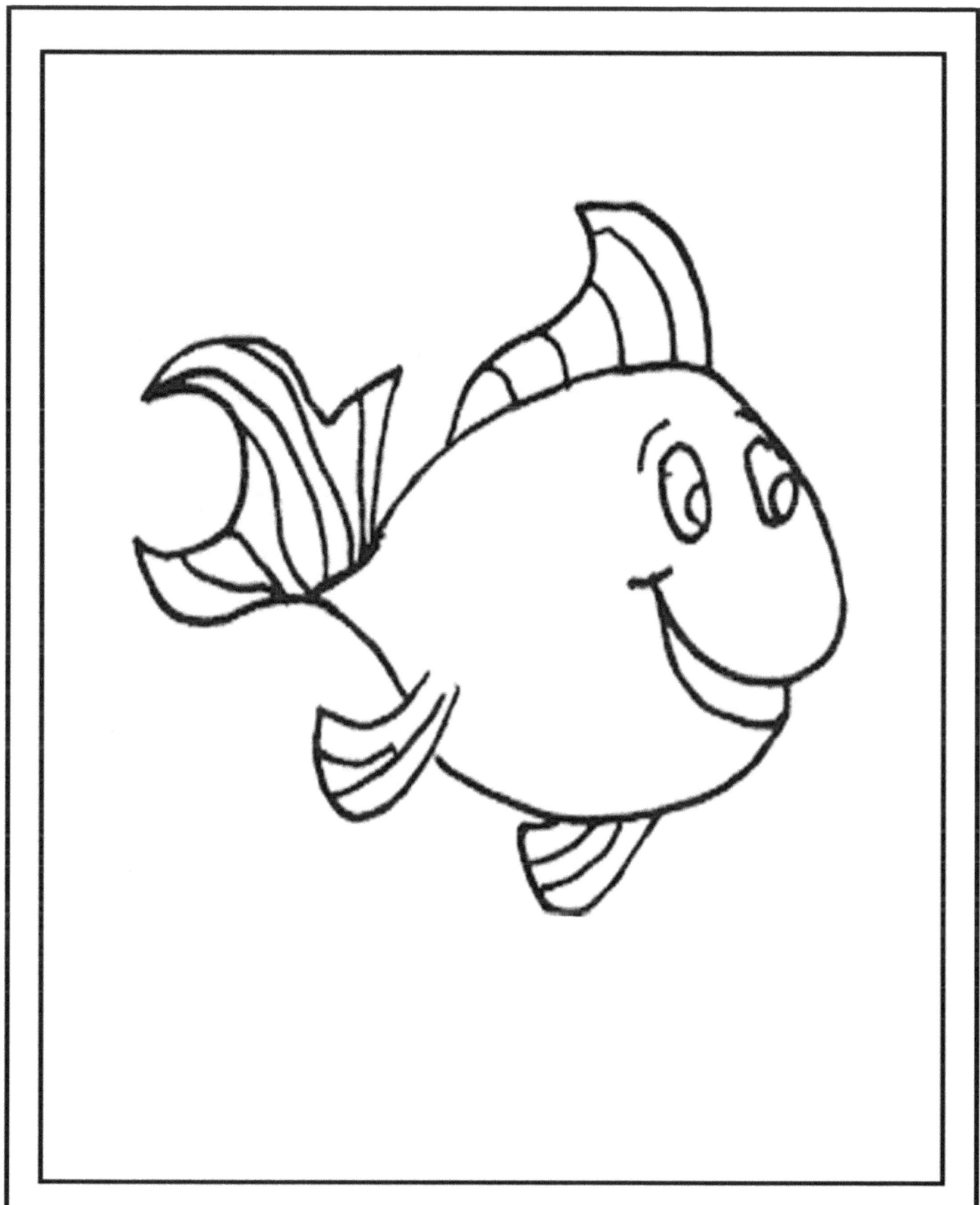

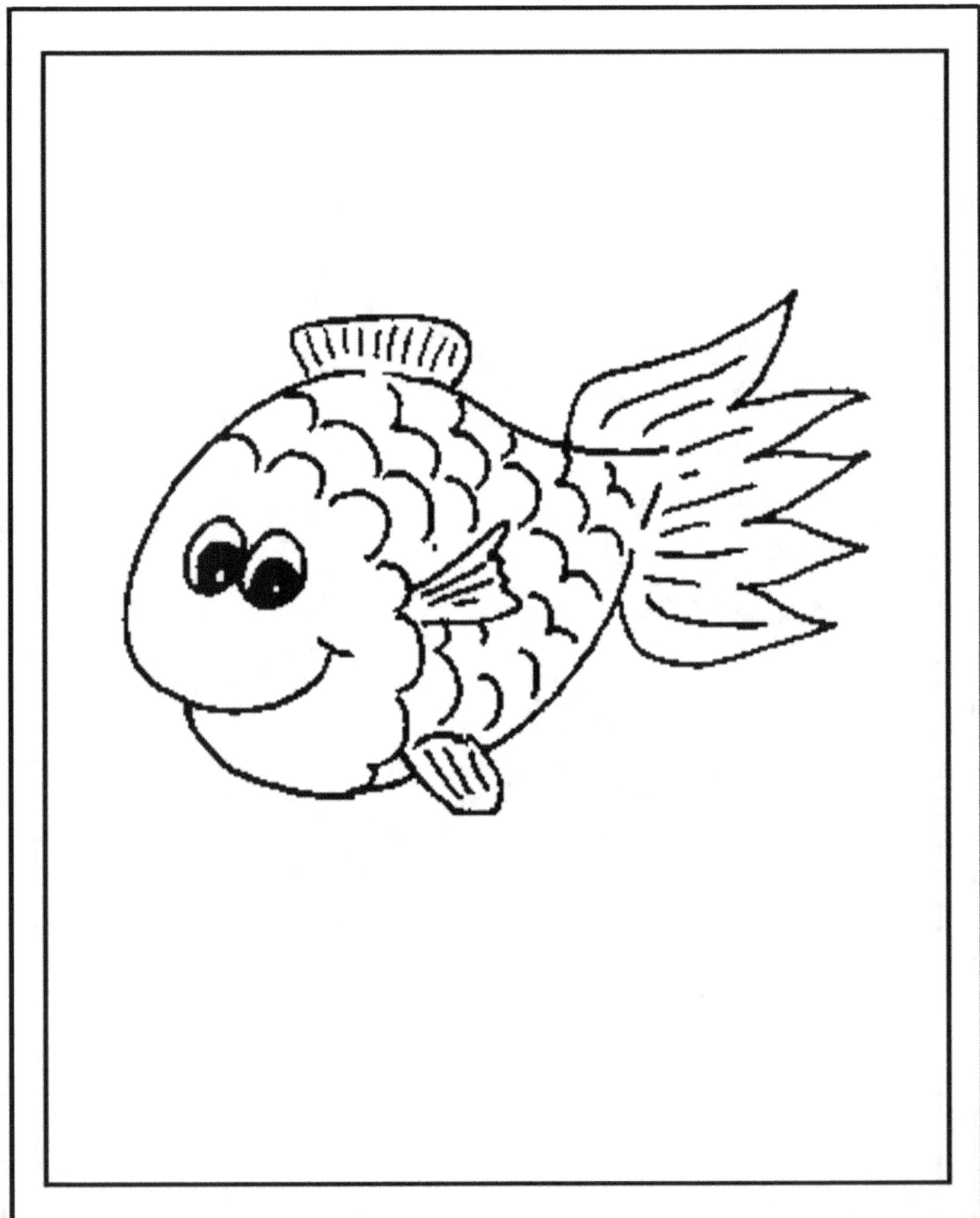

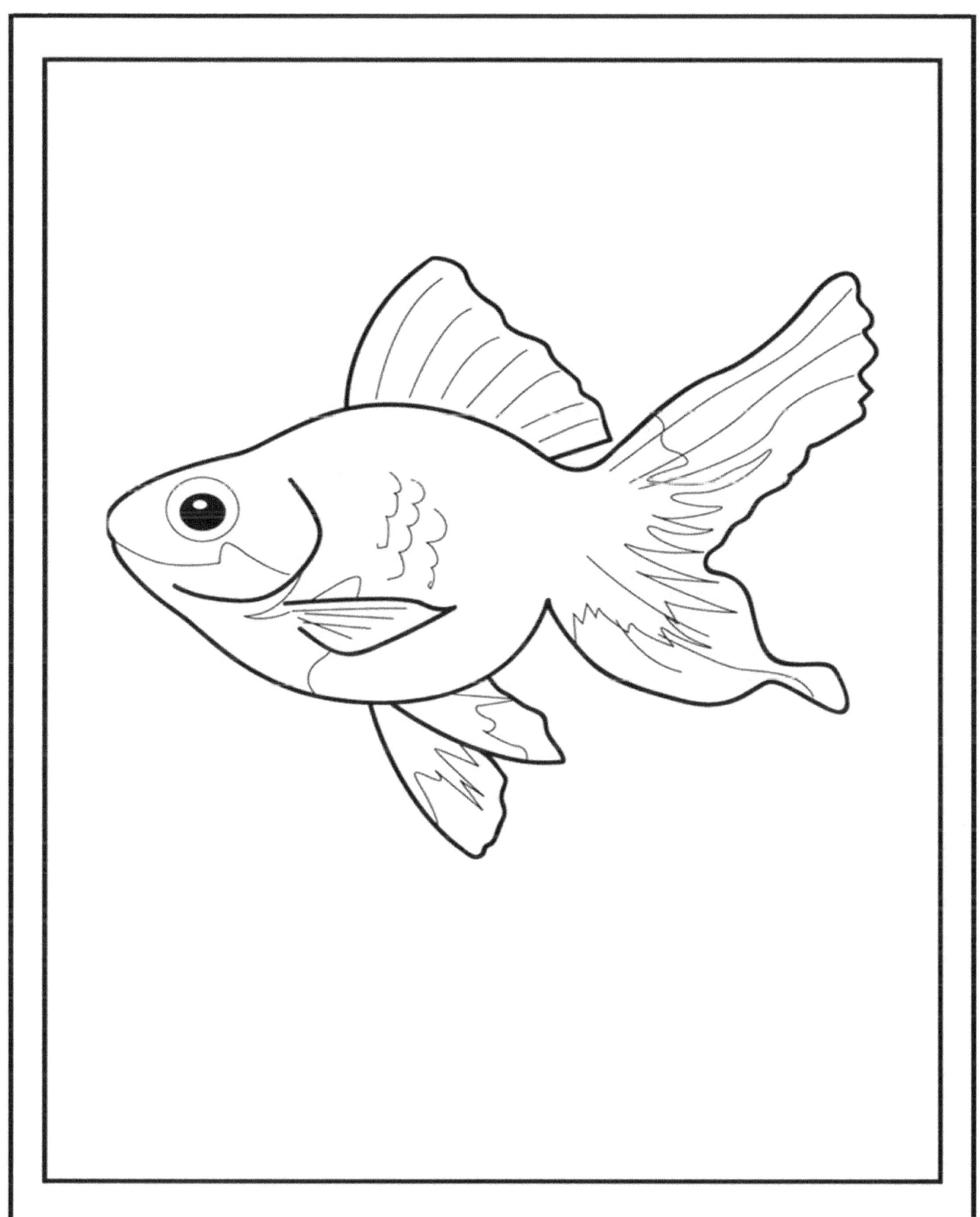

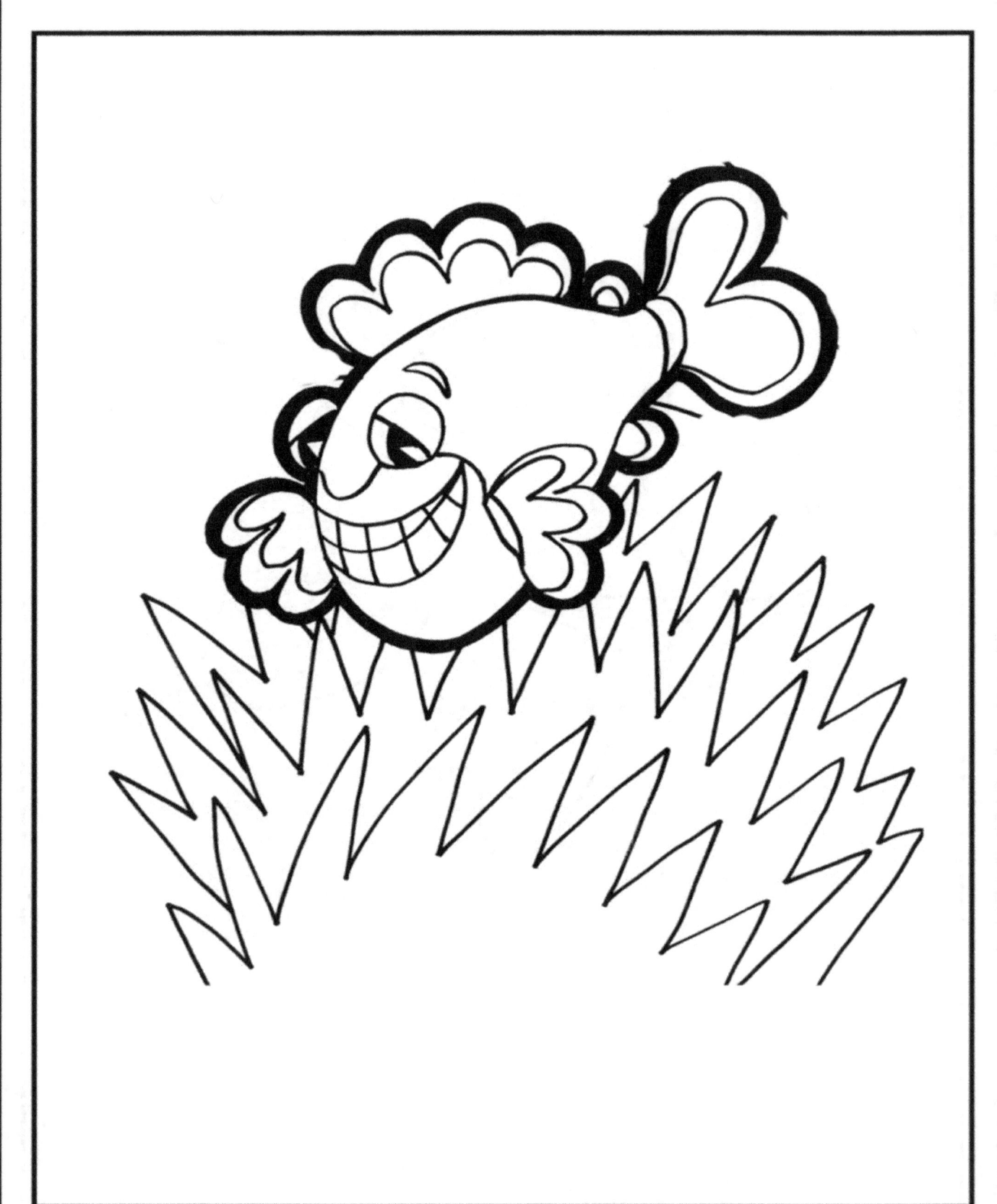

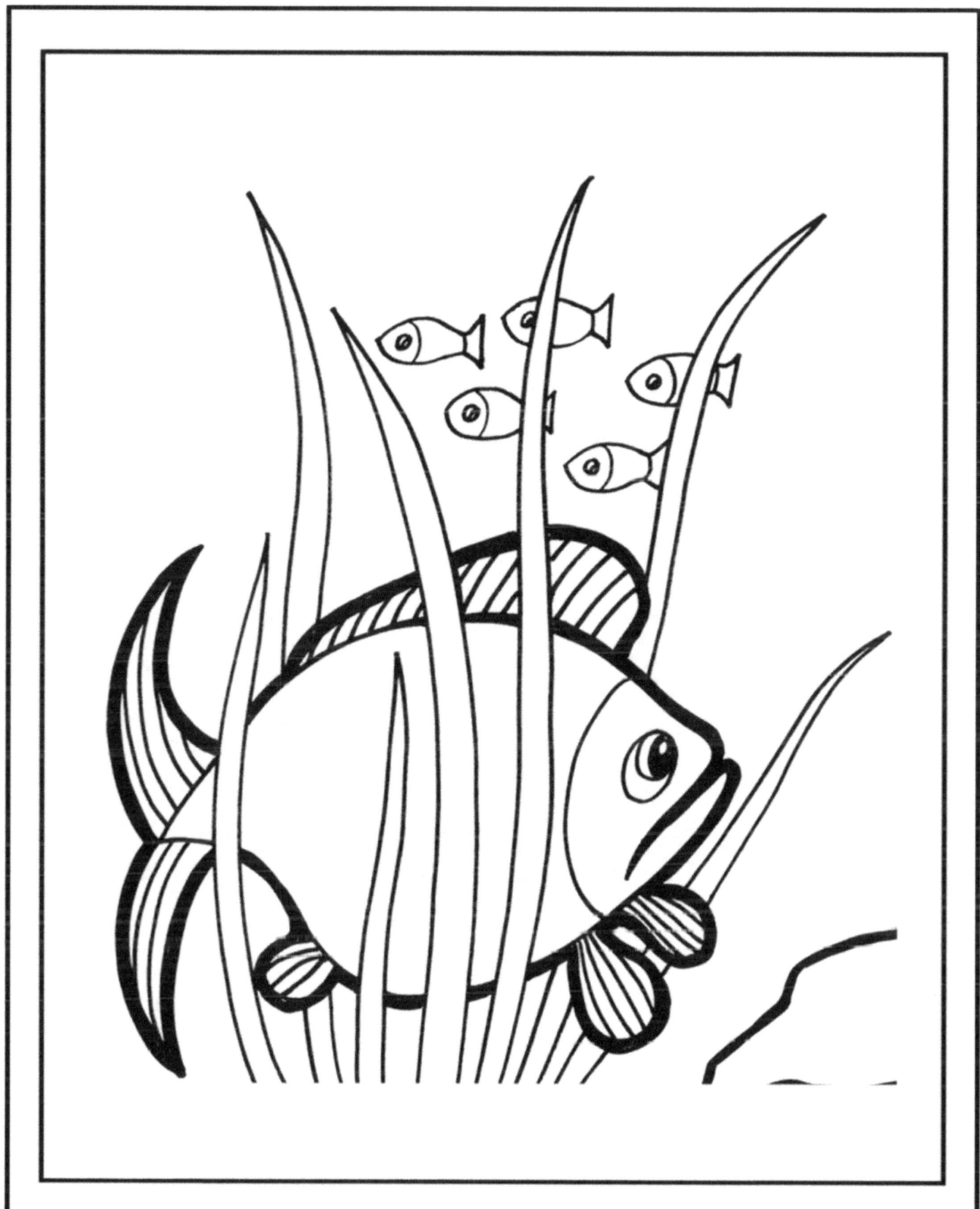

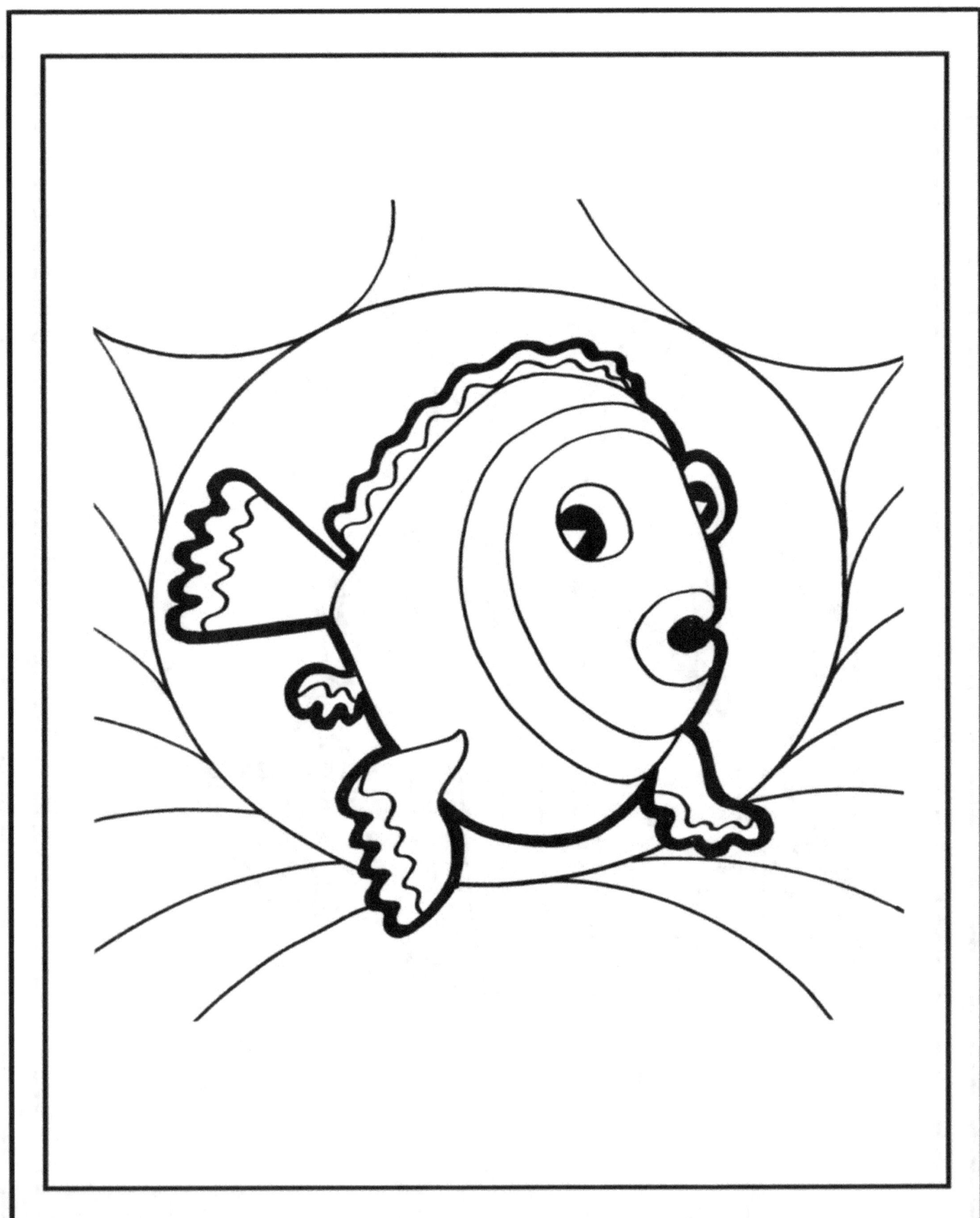

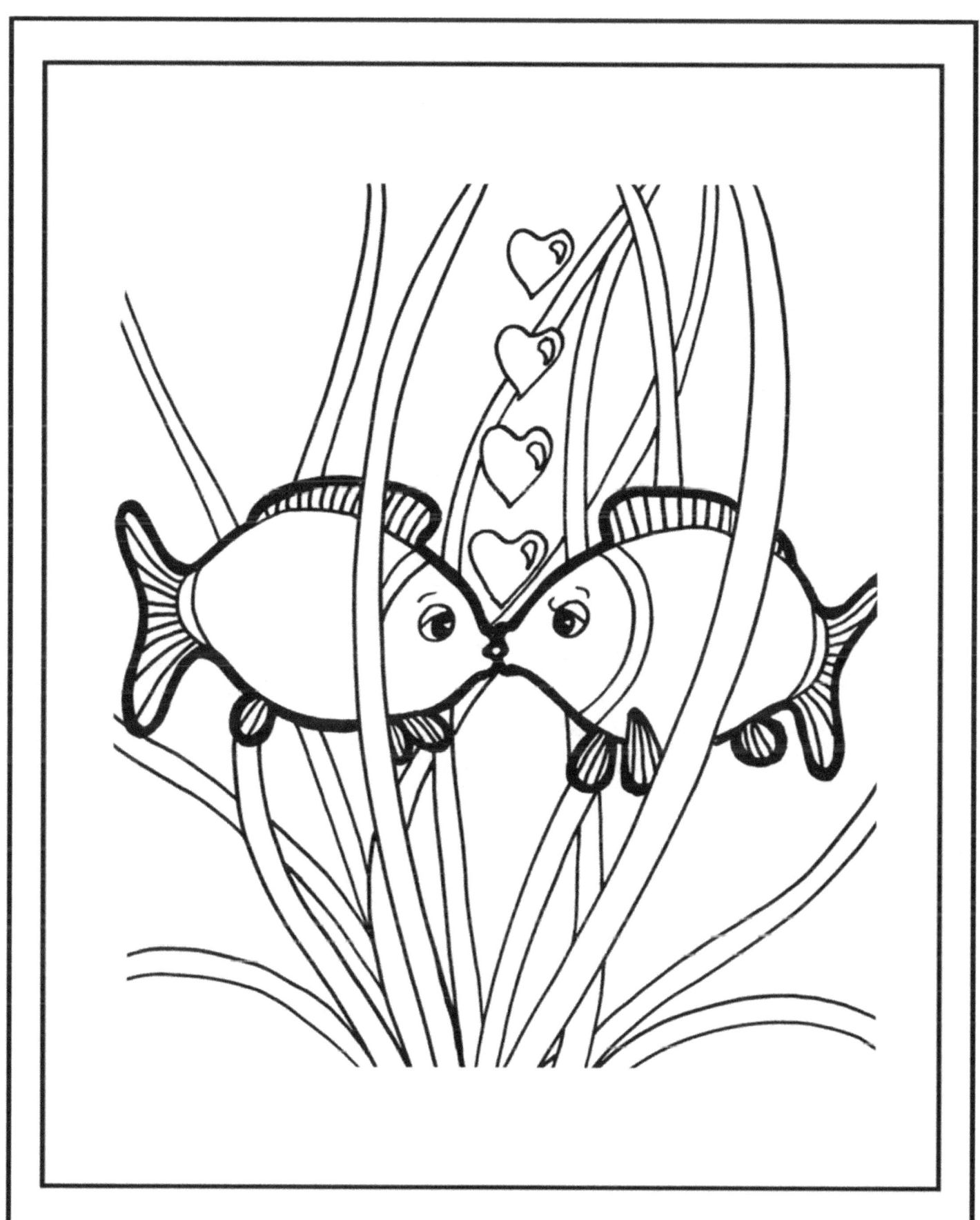

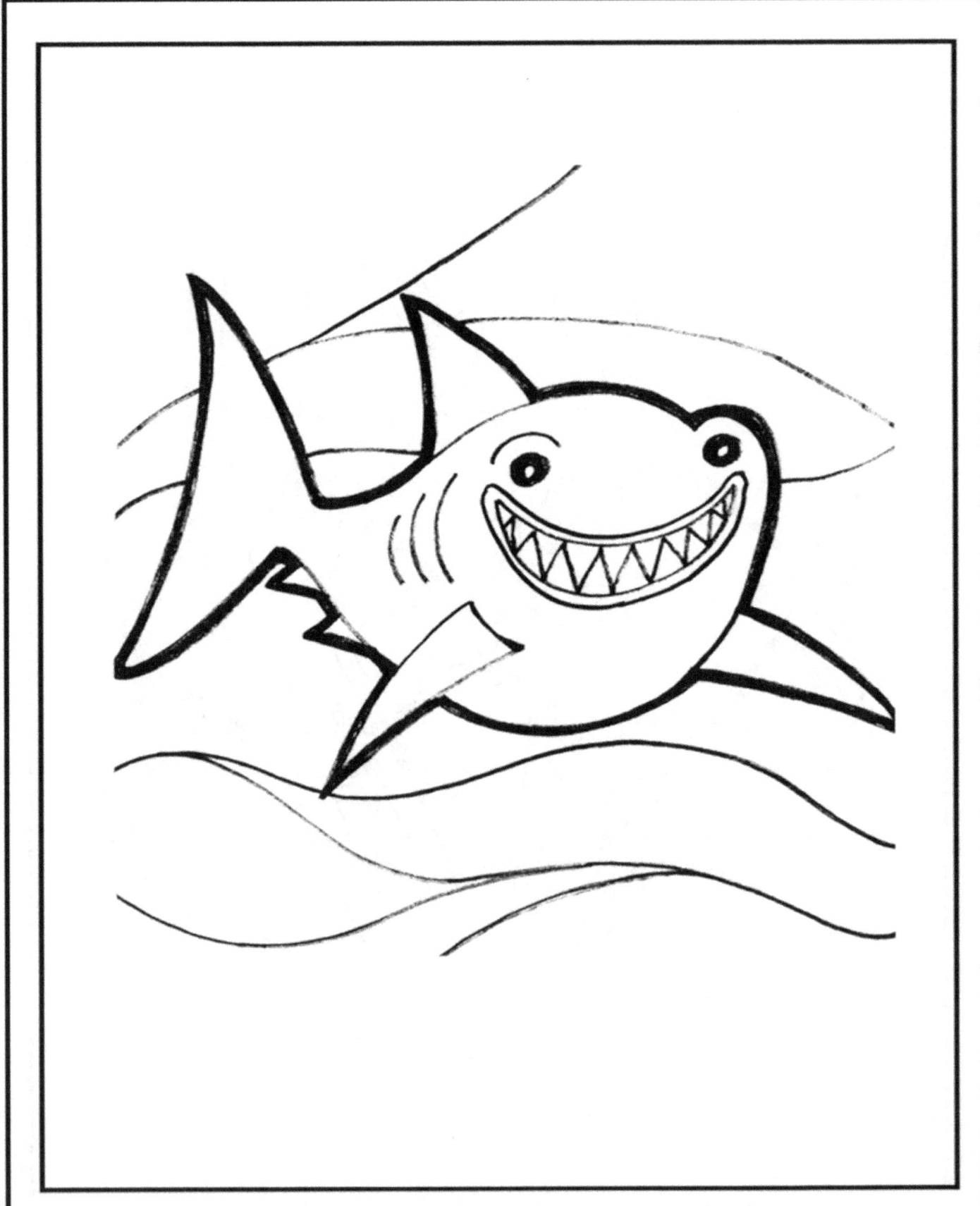

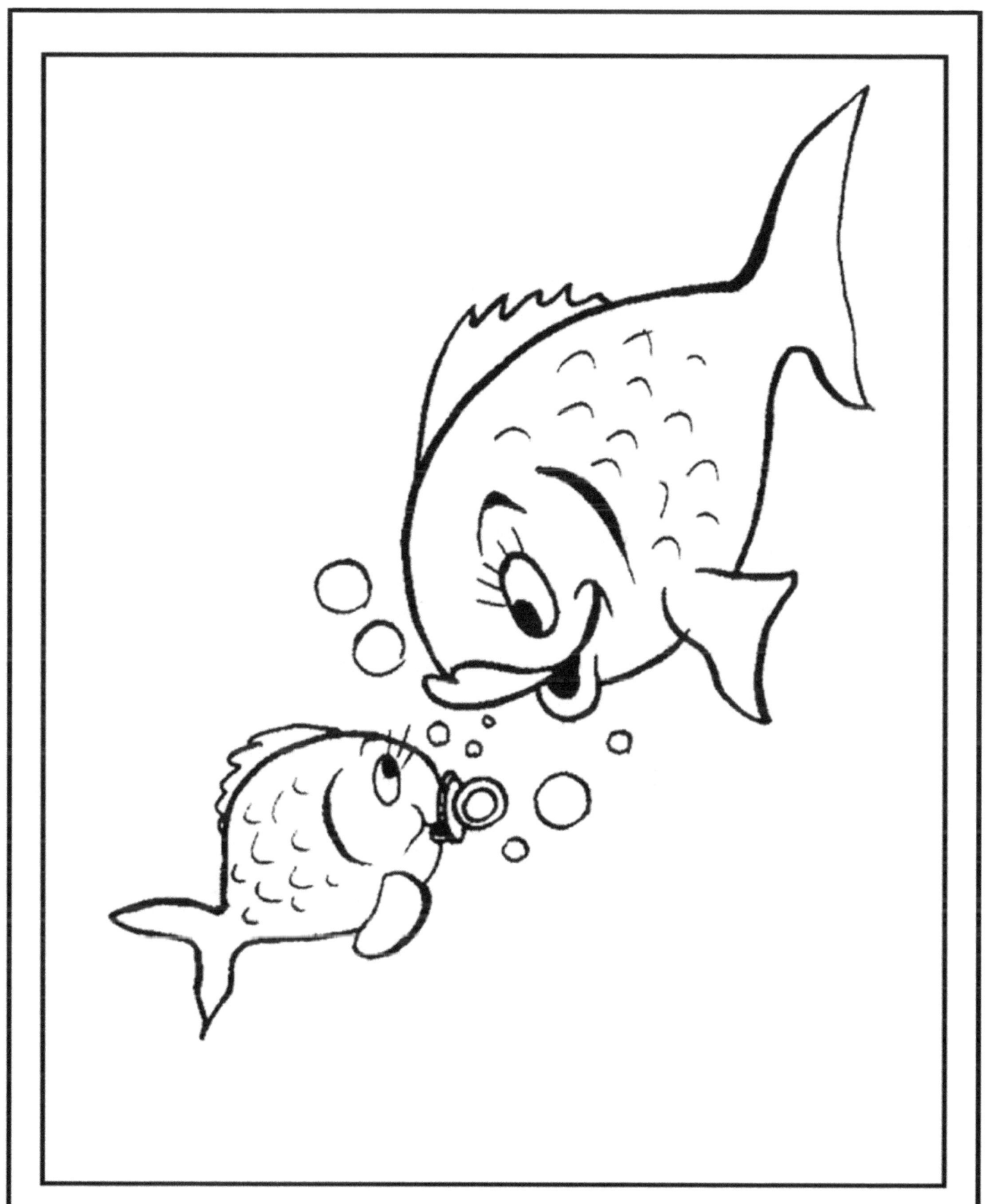

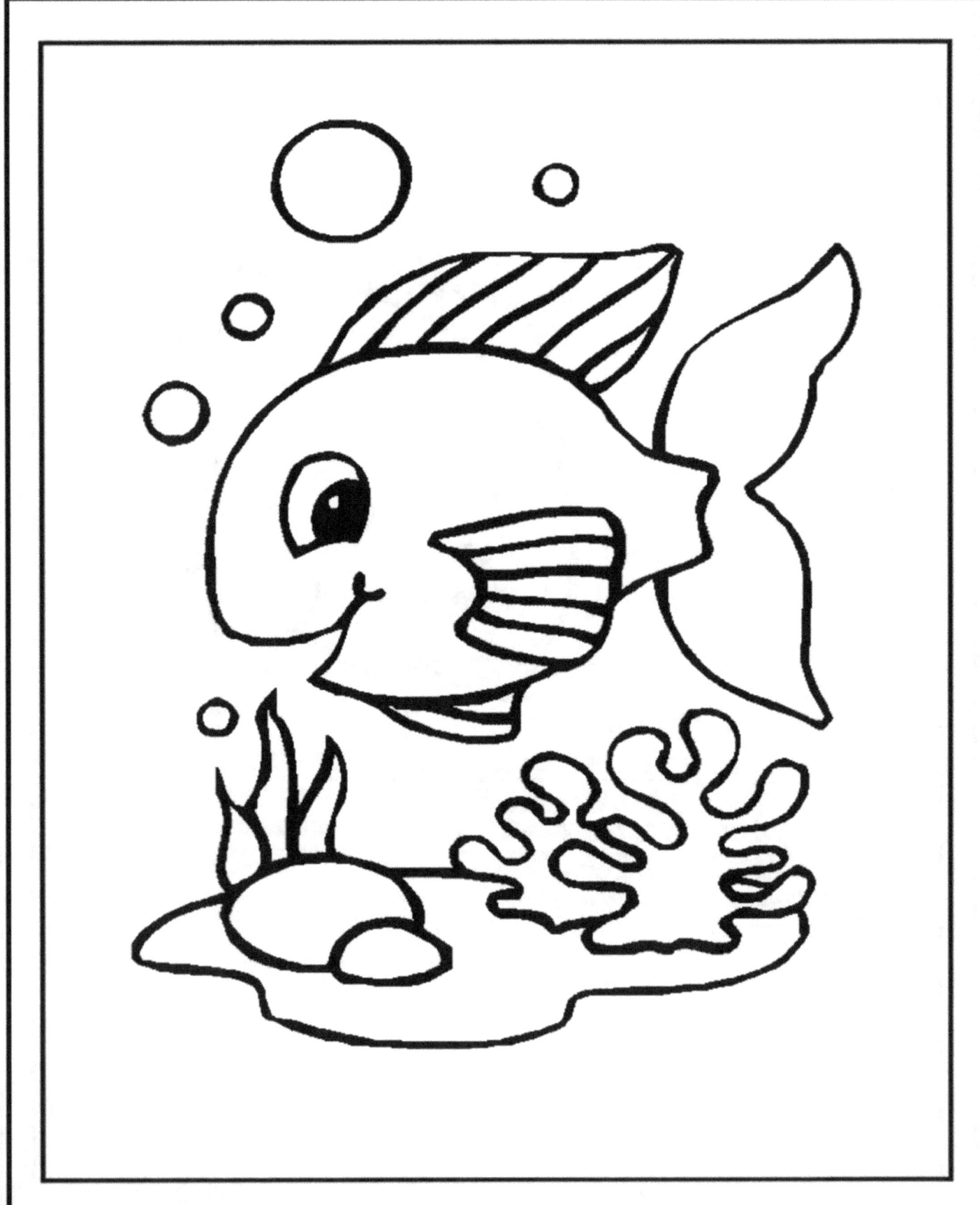

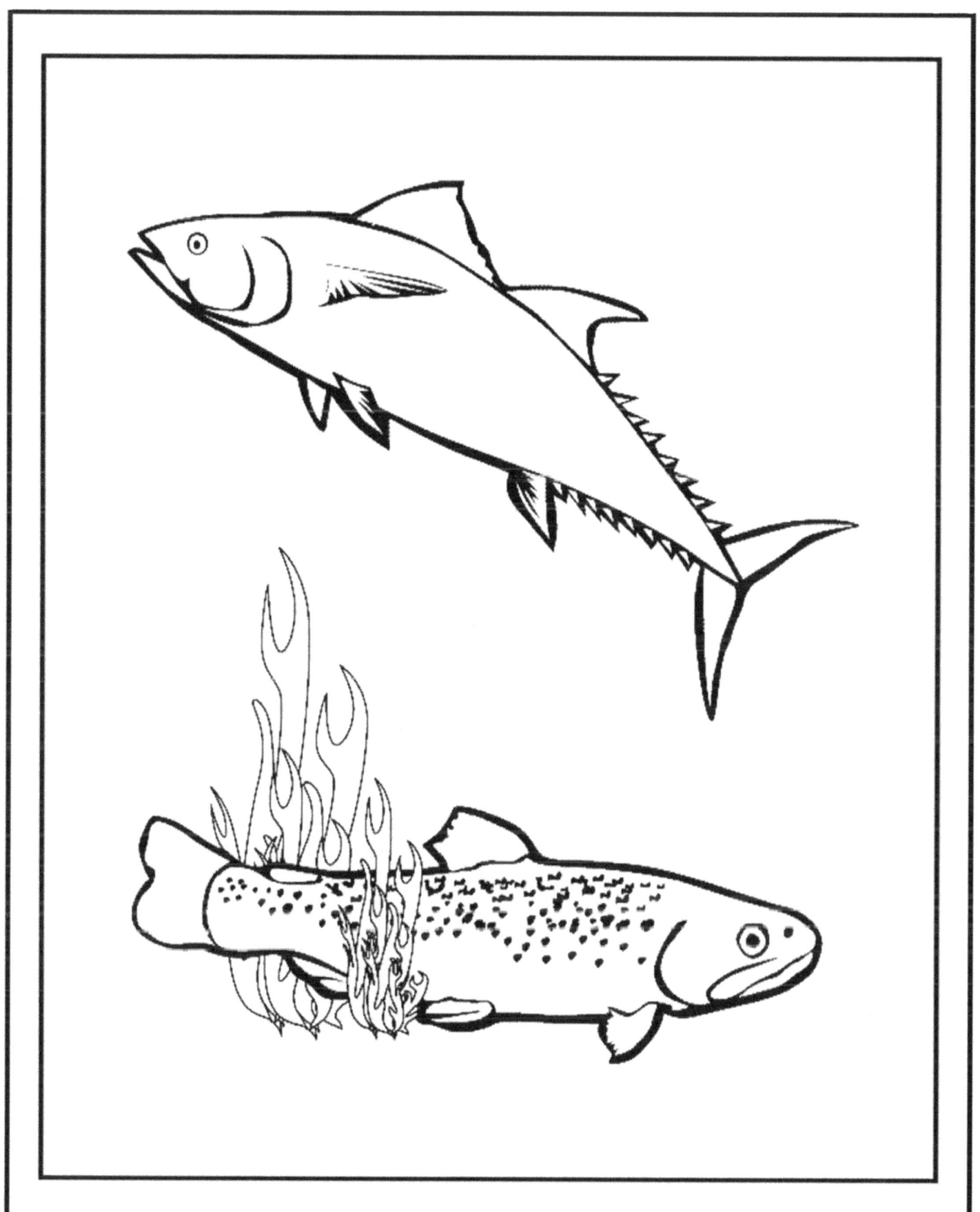

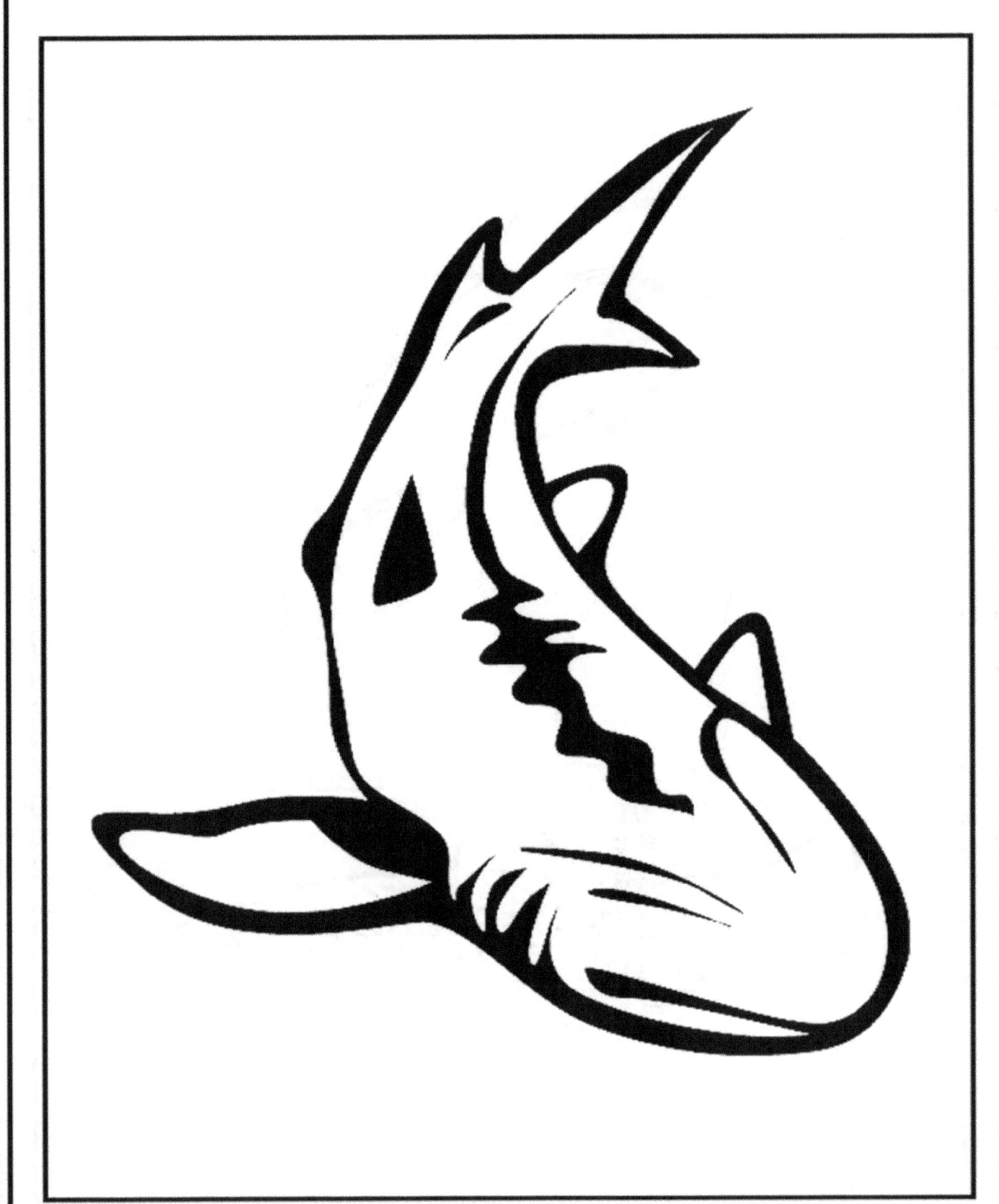

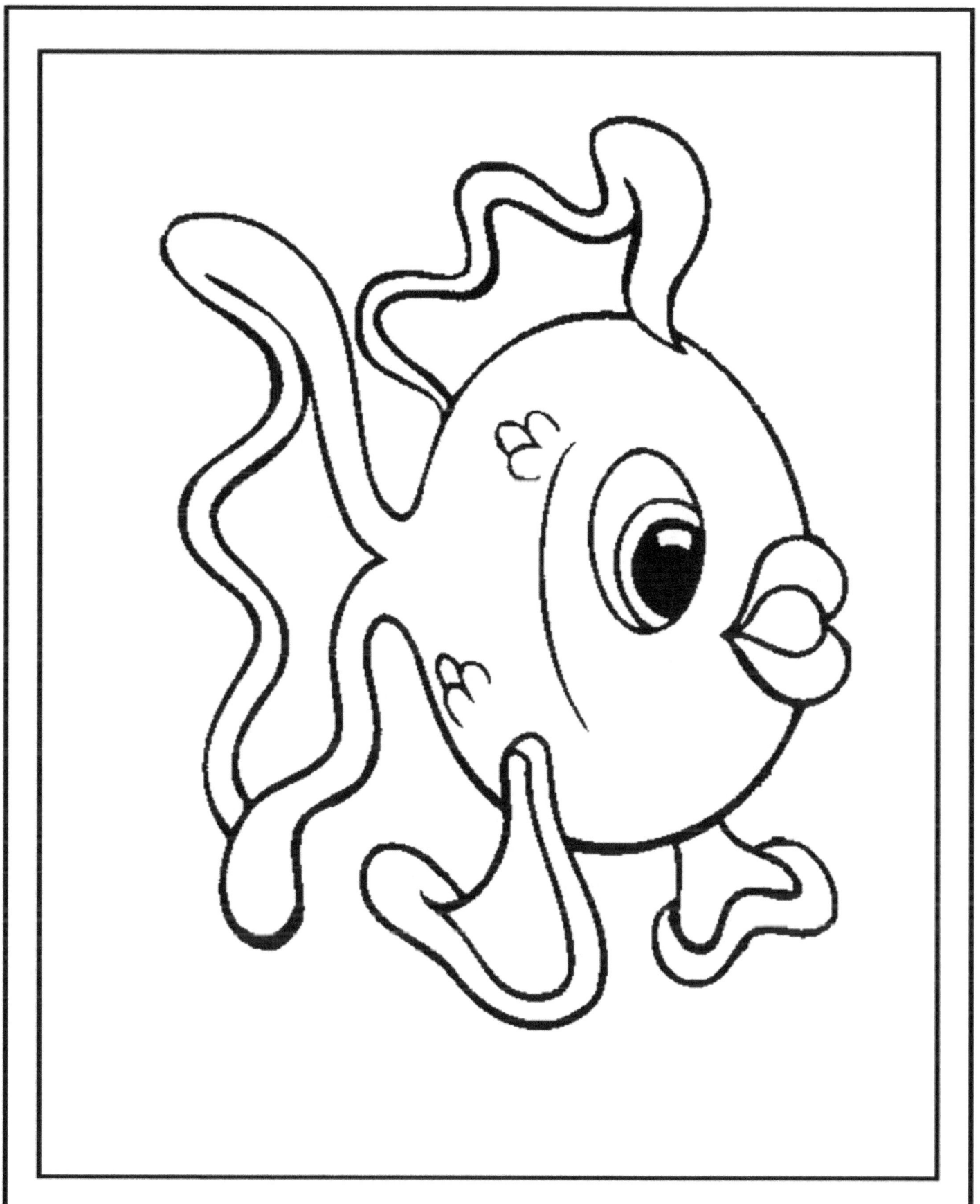

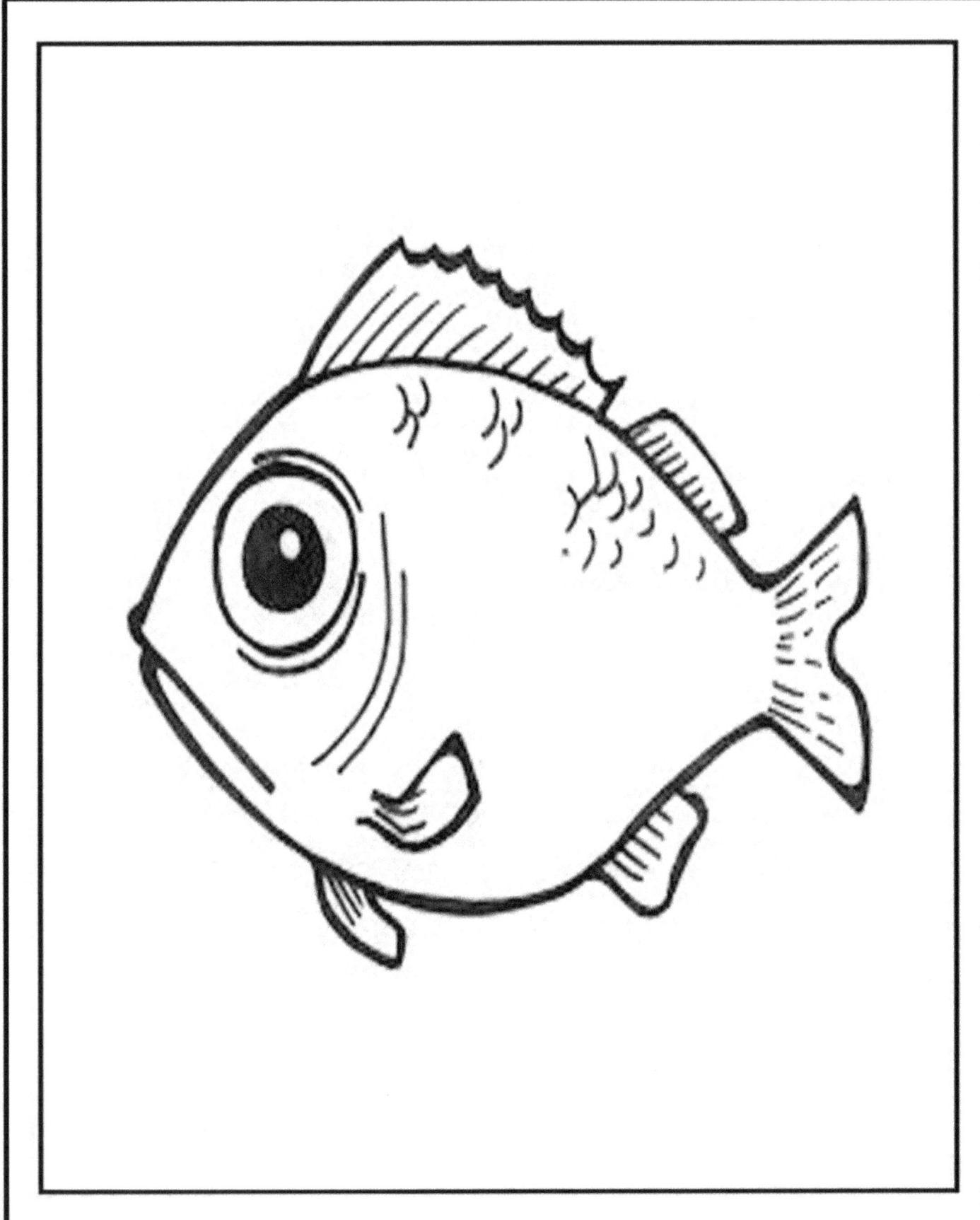

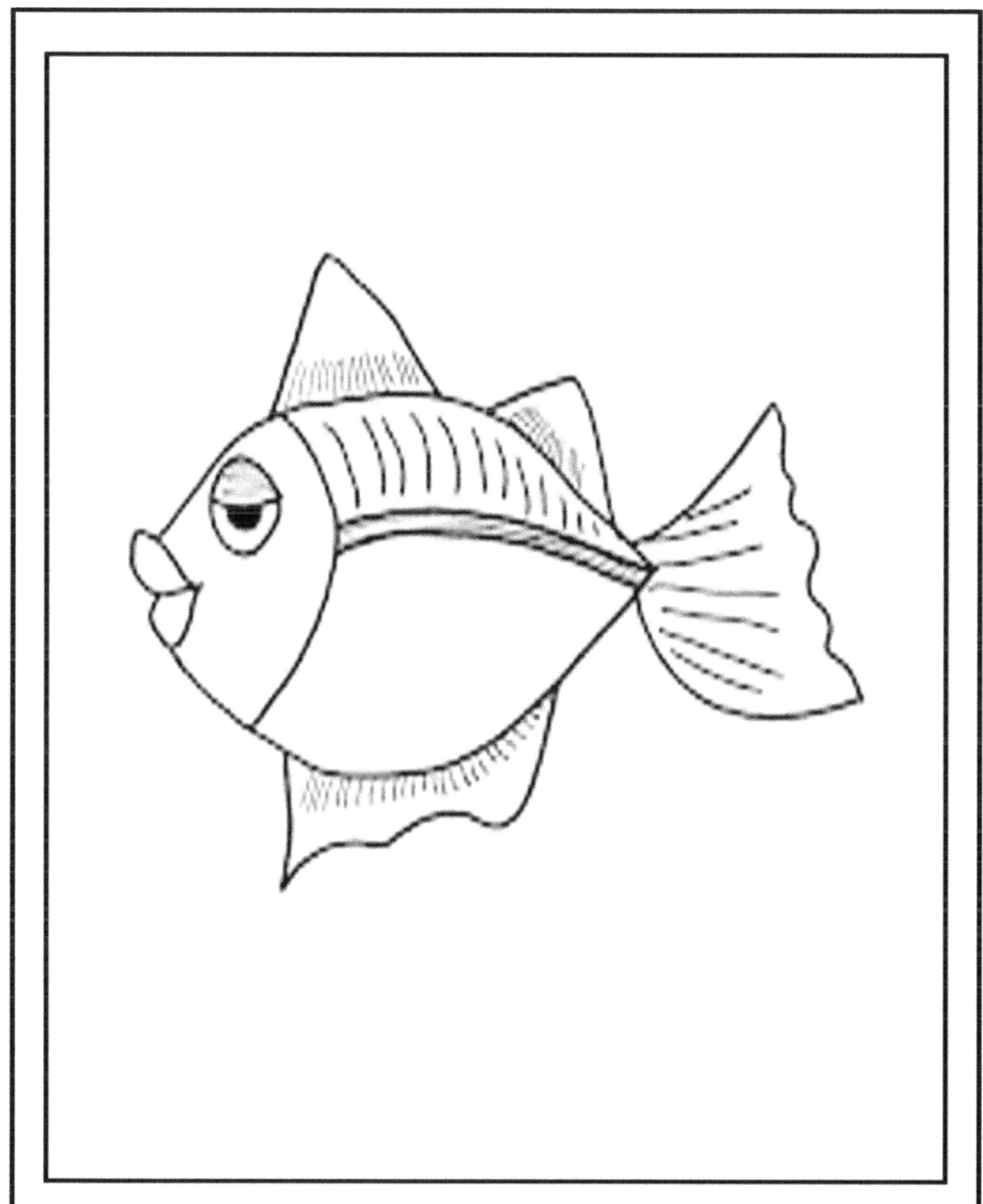

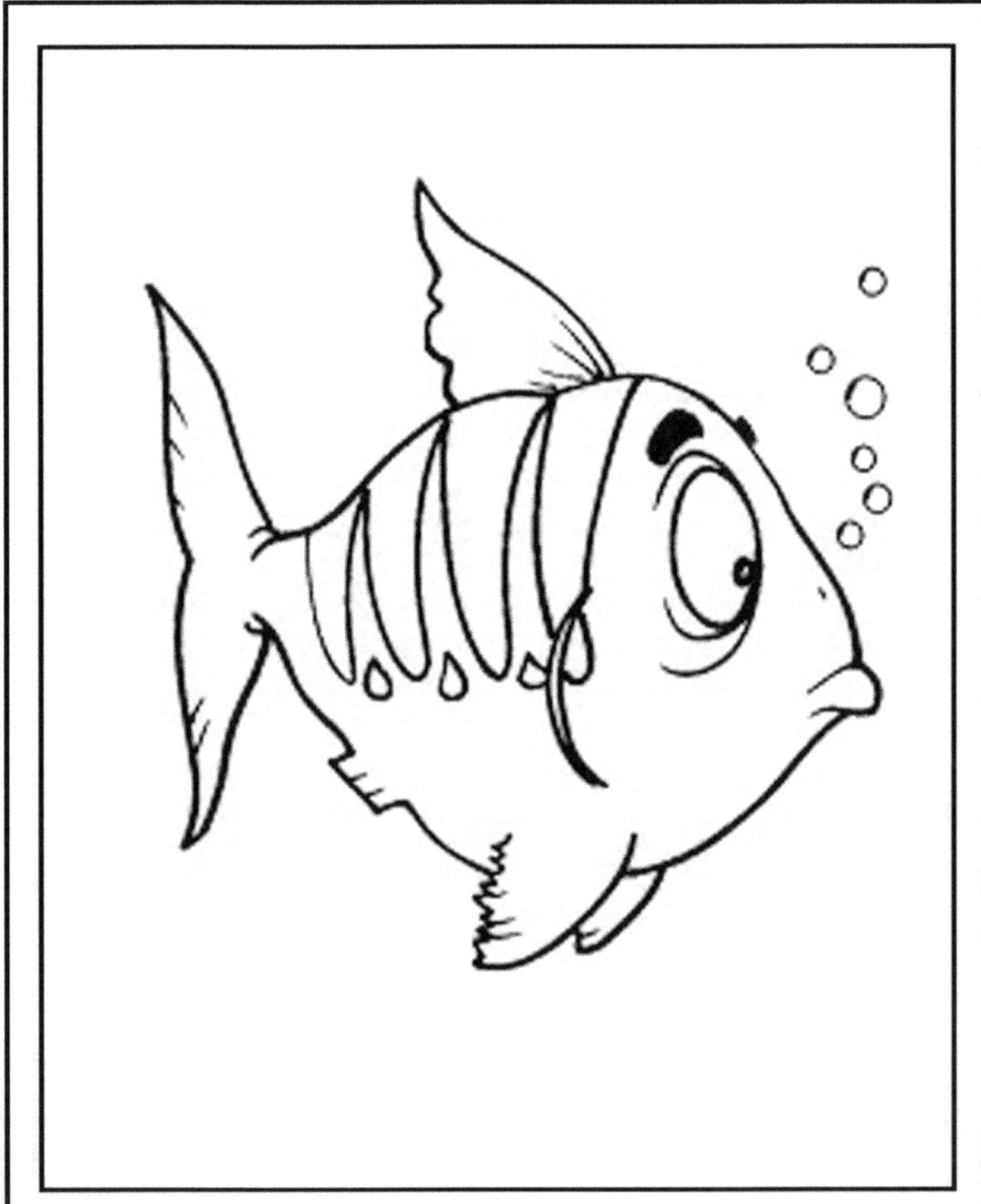

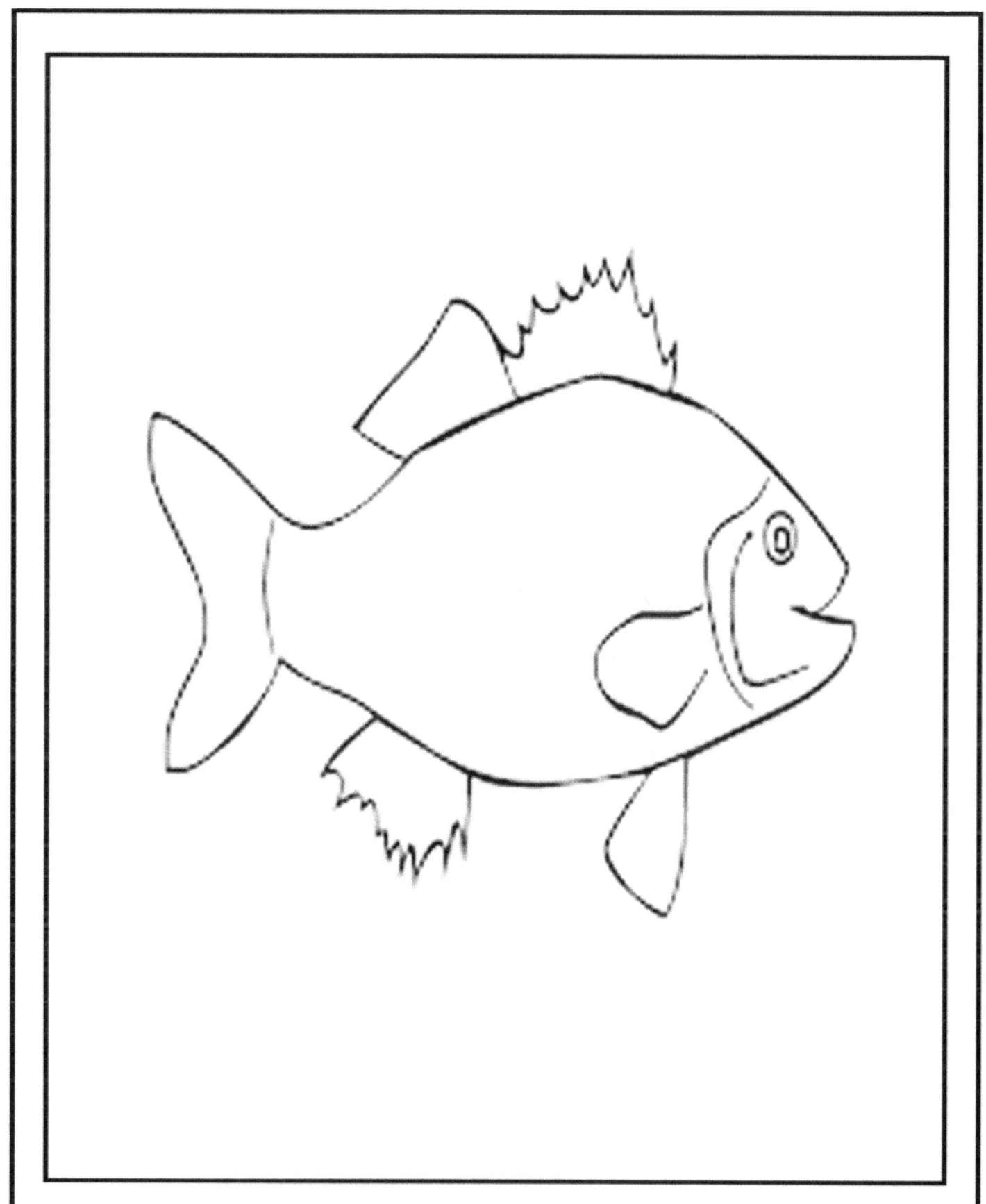

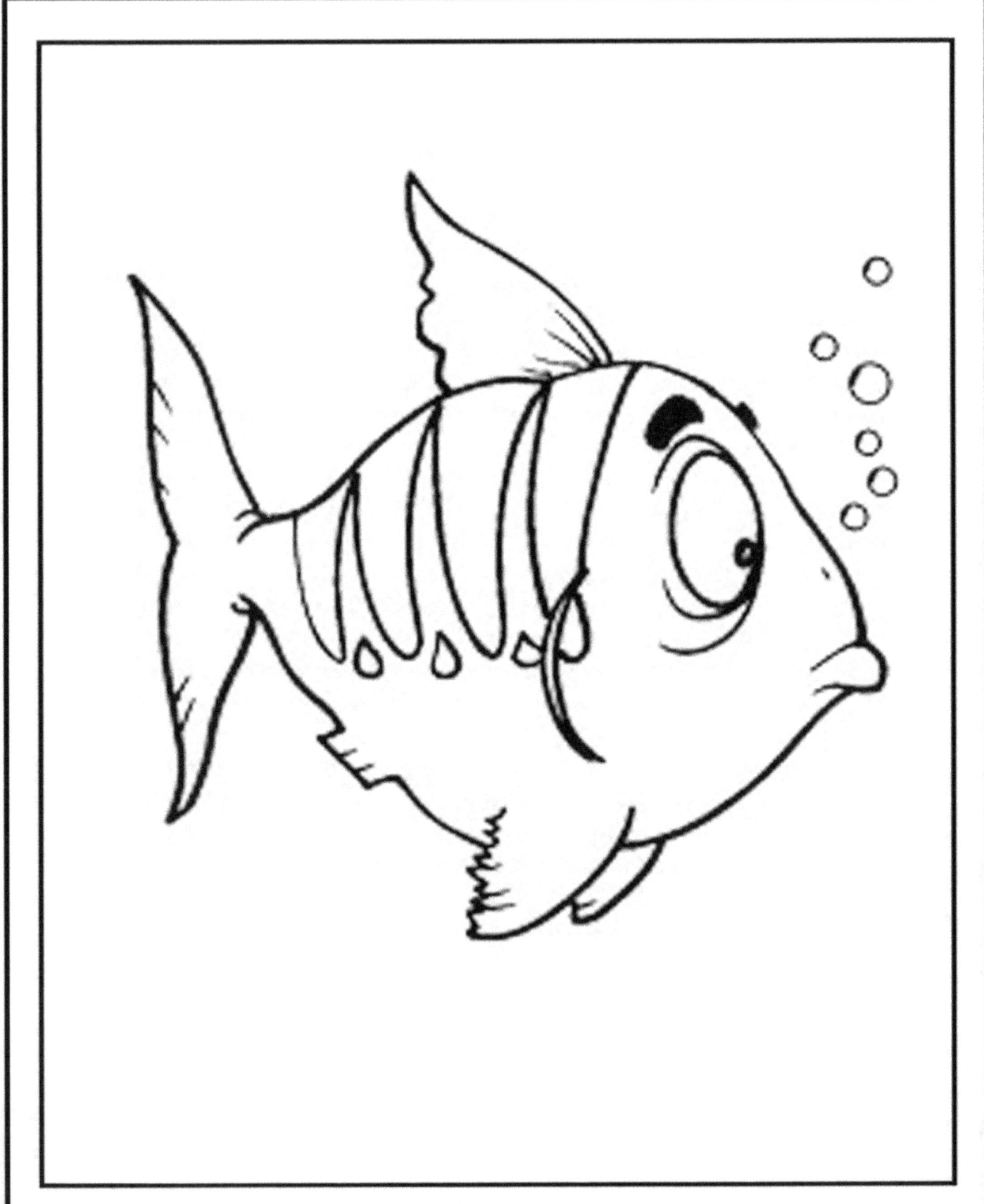

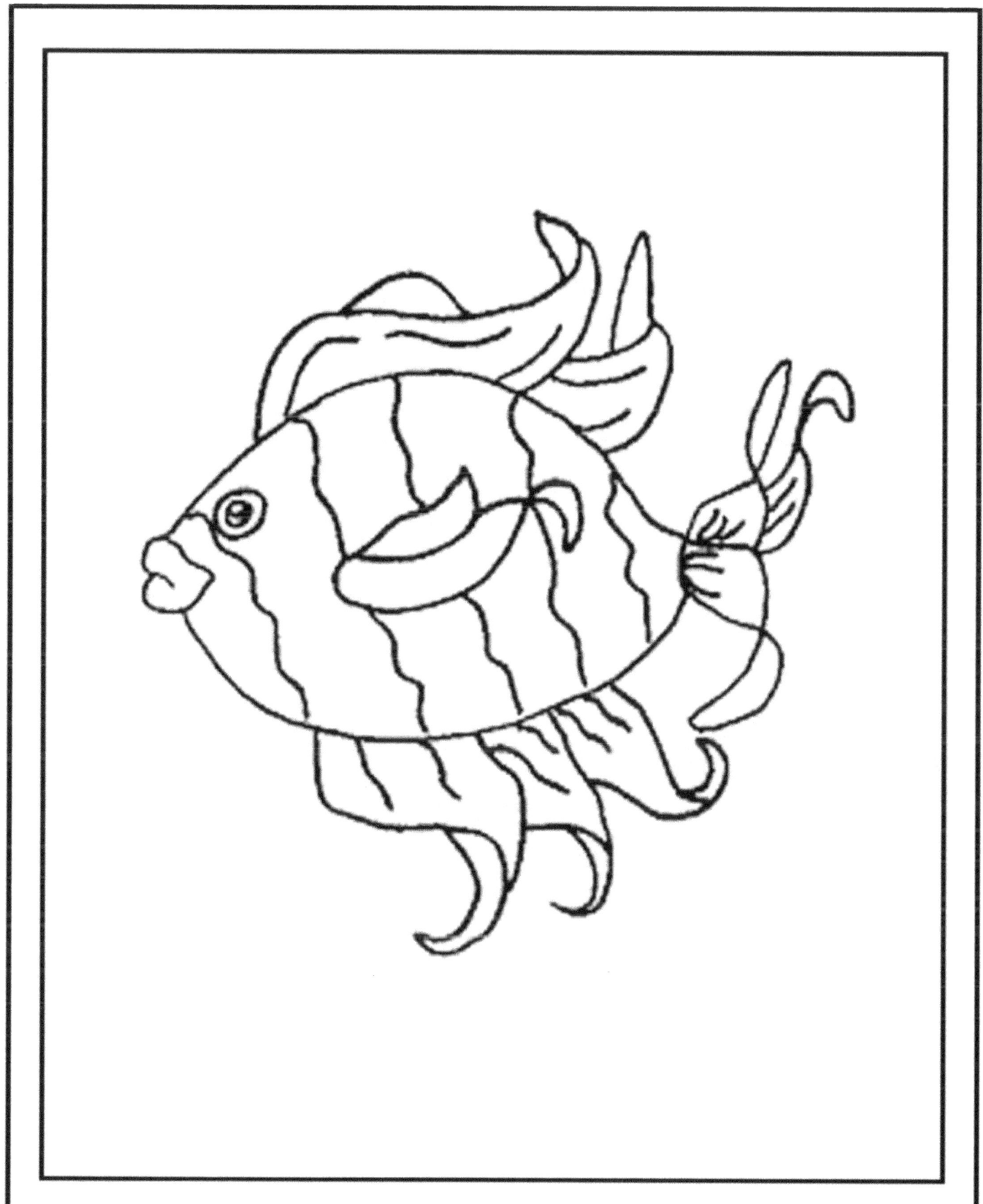

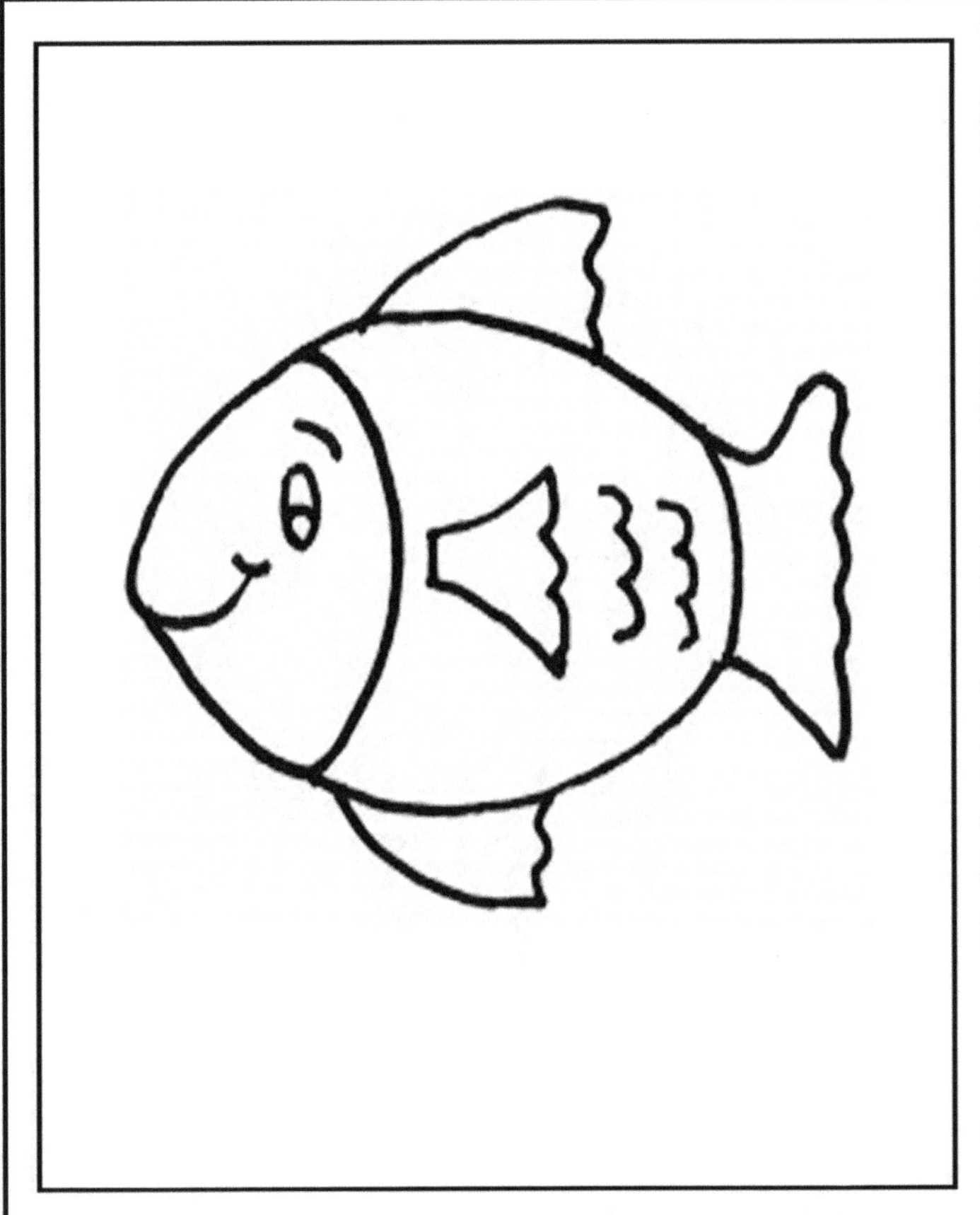

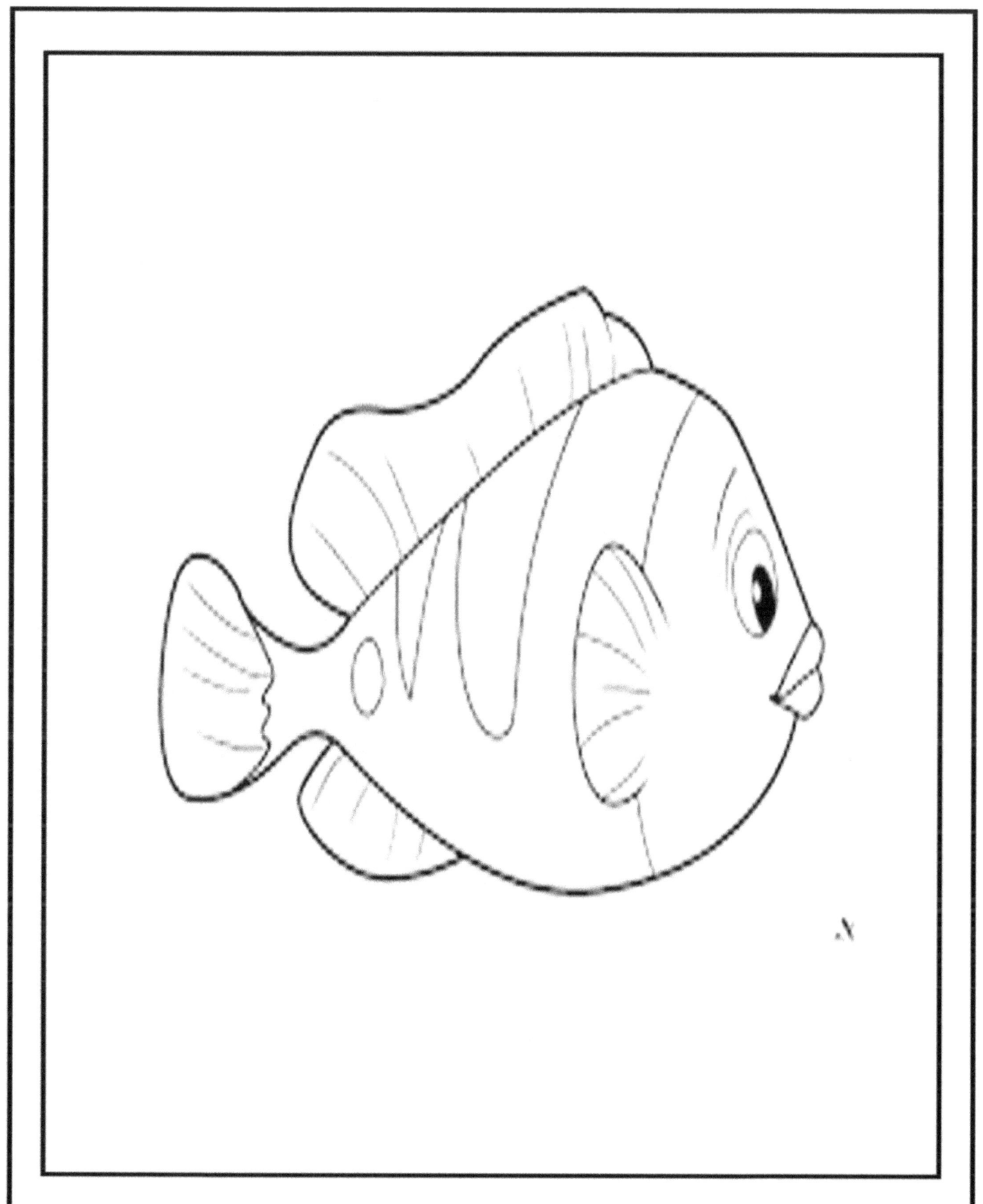

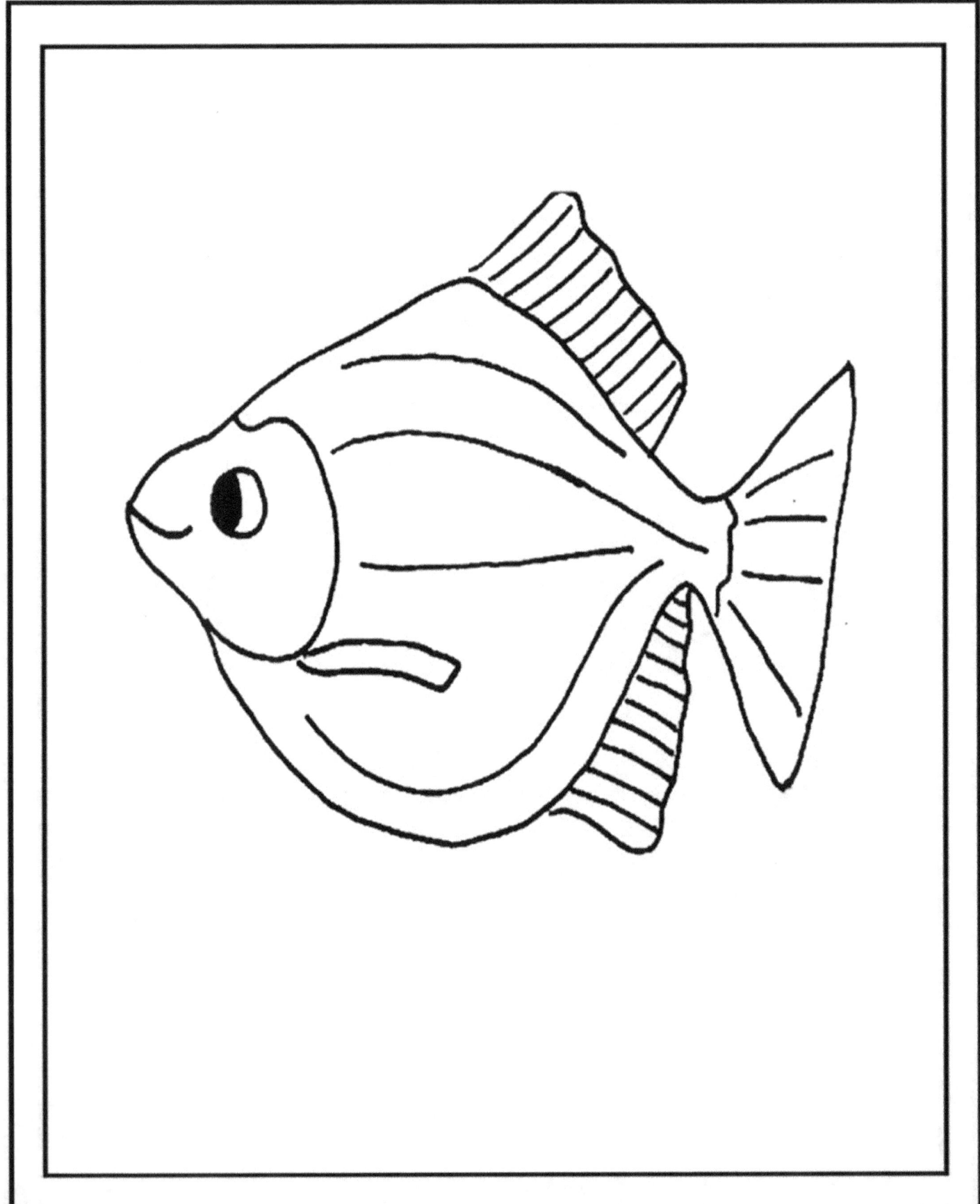

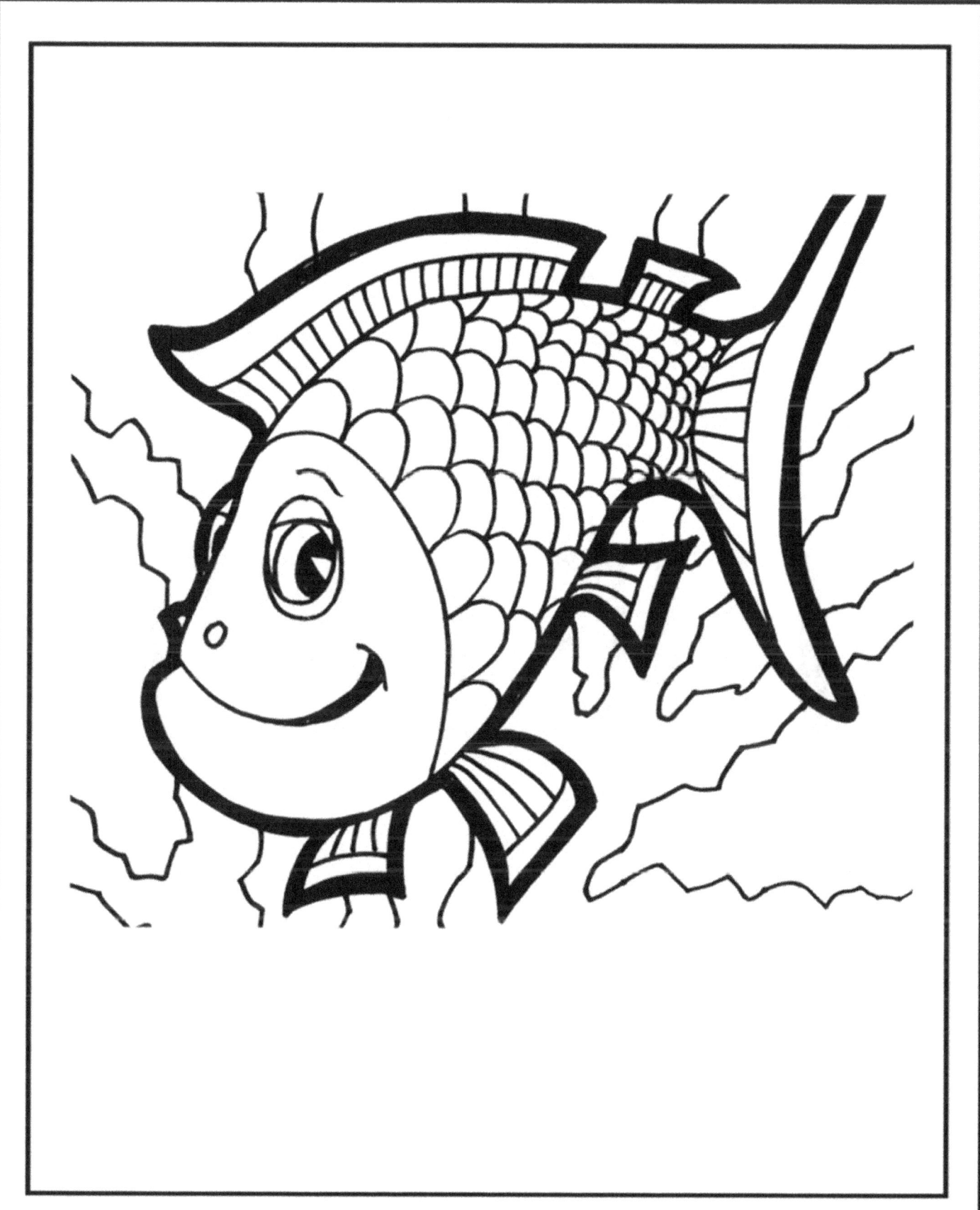

THE END